Moody Brain

Gauri Sood

This publication is in copyright. No part of this book may be reproduced or transmitted in any form or by any means without the written permission of the author.

Disclaimer: The information in this book is not intended to substitute a physician or therapist's advice or clinical care. Please consult your physician or health care provider if you are experiencing any symptoms or have questions pertaining to the information contained in this book.

Copyright © 2021 Gauri Sood

All rights reserved.

ISBN: 978-0-9995525-9-9

TO ALL THE PLANET'S CHILDREN

Moody Broody

HOW TO USE THIS BOOK

This book provides several practices to enhance mindfulness and happiness, and build resilience. Each section of this nine-part book has two pages:

The right page (with the image) describes the journey of Moody Broody. Please take cues from Broody to practice the skills he is learning.

The left page provides additional insights and practices, and space for you to write your thoughts.

The book is part of HappiGenius curriculum – an attention and resilience-centric approach to social and emotional learning (happigenius.com).

Disclaimer: The information in this book is not intended to substitute a physician or therapist's advice or clinical care. The book isn't intended to diagnose or treat any mental health disorder.

Part 1

Every brain wants to be happy.

But our brains can't be happy all the time.

All of the different feelings have a place in your life.

If you have a reason to be sad, then forcing happiness isn't the best idea.

Try your best to not get too sad though, and don't remain sad for too long.

Your thoughts:

In a little town lived a boy named Broody.

Most days he felt a little moody.

Part 2

Some brains find it easier to be happier.

However, every brain can learn happiness skills.

These skills make your brain happier by changing its wiring.

When you're happier, you feel better and even become healthier.

Your teachers and parents can help you apply happiness skills in your life.

Your thoughts:

One spring day, a new sub came to the school.

She showed him tricks, how to be cool.

Part 3

Curiosity is a great source of happiness.

Notice the world around you to increase your curiosity.

Become curious about all the different sounds around you.

Pause at this moment and carefully listen to the sounds in your room.

You might hear the hum of a fan, someone's voice, or a car in the distance.

Your thoughts:

Notice the details in the world around.

Turn your ears, to the quietest sound.

Part 4

Look at this image and count the stars.

Try and discover familiar shapes in the clouds.

Notice all the colors in your home and classroom.

Look around in a familiar space and notice at least one new detail.

It could be a scratch on the wall, a pattern on the rug, or a box of crayons.

Your thoughts:

Count the stars, up in the sky.

Name the colors, on the butterfly.

Part 5

The more you notice, the more you remember.

How many phone numbers have you memorized?

Find your state on this map (if you live in the U.S.).

Do you remember the license plate number of your car?

Try to remember exactly what you ate for dinner yesterday.

Your thoughts:

Learn to remember, teensy little more.

Where on the map is Baltimore?

Part 6

Try and find all the letters (A to Z) in your home.

Try and find all the numbers (1 to 10) in your classroom.

Pay attention to all the different color cars you see on a drive.

Can you find five groups of four in the image here (e.g., four burners)?

Recall all the things you see as you travel from your home to the school.

Your thoughts:

Search in your home, for the number four.

Part 7

Read the names of these dinosaurs.

Which dinosaur is your personal favorite?

Try to memorize the full names of two dinosaurs.

Can you create a story that features these two dinosaurs?

Try to find similarities and differences between any two dinosaurs.

Your thoughts:

Come let's spell, your favorite dinosaur!

Part 8

Each breath fills your body with good energy.

When you breathe deep and slow, you become calm.

When you are calm, you become happier and can focus better.

Practice deep and slow breathing for at least five breaths every day.

Become calm with each breath in and let out strain with each breath out.

Your thoughts:

Breathe deep and slow, it calms your brain

Breathe in peace, breathe out your strain.

Part 9

Let life's little things make you happy.

Be happy when you eat good food and have a friend to play with.

The kinder you are to others and yourself, the happier you will be.

Feel grateful for both the small and large things that you get in life.

Being grateful doesn't mean that life is perfect; it just means you have enough reasons to be thankful in this moment.

Your thoughts:

Your bucket of happy feelings, make sure it is full.

Act kind, be calm, and feel grateful.

What new skills did Broody learn from the substitute teacher that made him happier? Write your thoughts here:

The kinder you are and the more thankful,

the smaller your frown, the more you're cool!

Broody learned the following from the new teacher:

- It's okay to be sad once in a while
- He can train his brain to become happier
- Three steps to making his brain happier are:
    - Become more curious and notice the world
    - Practice deep breathing to calm your mind
    - Feel grateful for little things and be kind to everyone

Twenty years later…

Broody is a grown up now.

Most of the days he feels happy.

Guess what he does for a living?

He teaches kids how to be happier!

Moody Broody

Coloring Pages

Moody Broody

ACKNOWLEDGMENTS

I am grateful to all my friends and family for their love and support, especially my dad, Amit Sood. I am also grateful to every person who is passionate about and working to build a kinder, happier, and stronger world for all of our planet's children.

ABOUT THE AUTHOR

Gauri Sood is a bright and creative high school student. She is the co-creator and lead instructor of the HappiGenius curriculum.

Moody Broody is part of the HappiGenius curriculum, a program designed to help enhance young children's focus, social skills, resilience, and positive emotions.

For more information, please visit happigenius.com.

Made in the USA
Middletown, DE
06 January 2022